THE "FAITH IN

General Editors: Geoffrey H

TRIAL OF FAITH

THE STORY OF RICHARD WURMBRAND

R. J. Owen

THE RELIGIOUS EDUCATION PRESS

A Member of the Pergamon Group
HEADINGTON HILL HALL · OXFORD

Pergamon Press Ltd, Headington Hill Hall, Oxford OX3 0BW
Pergamon Press Inc., Maxwell House, Fairview Park, Elmsford,
   New York 10523
Pergamon of Canada Ltd, 207 Queen's Quay West, Toronto 1
Pergamon Press (Aust.) Pty Ltd, 19a Boundary Street
   Rushcutters Bay, N.S.W. 2011, Australia

First edition 1974

Printed in Great Britain by A. Wheaton & Co. Exeter

ISBN 0 08 017608 9 non-net
ISBN 0 08 017609 7 net

TRIAL OF FAITH

The story of Richard Wurmbrand

It was Sunday, 29 February, 1948. Pastor Wurmbrand was on his way to church. Suddenly a black Ford car belonging to the Rumanian secret police stopped in front of him. Two men jumped out and dragged him into the car; a third man pointed a gun at him while a fourth drove the car quickly away. Yes, this Christian minister had been kidnapped—not by terrorists, but by the State Police.

He was taken to the headquarters of the secret police. His identity papers, belongings, tie ànd shoelaces were taken from him. His name was also taken from him. He was told that he would be called Vasile Georgescu. This was done so that Richard's relations and friends would find it difficult to trace him. Then he was put in prison.

Why did this all happen? Who was Richard Wurmbrand? What was his crime? To understand all these things it is necessary to go back to his childhood, and follow the varied events which led to that fateful moment when he was arrested in 1948.

No God

Richard was born a year or so before the First World War began. His father died when he was nine years old, and after that the family was always short of money and often had very little food.

He was brought up by Jewish parents, but they had no liking for their religion. Yet religion interested him. Once he went into a synagogue, a kind of Jewish church, and saw a man he knew praying for the recovery of his daughter who was very ill. She died the next day. Later · Richard met the man's minister, the rabbi.

"How is it possible for a loving God to refuse such a prayer?" he asked.

The rabbi could not explain. Richard found it hard to believe in a God who let so many people suffer. He found it even harder to believe that a person like Jesus Christ ever lived.

Not surprisingly, by the time he was fourteen he already believed there was no God. He occasionally went to church, but he did not know why. He did not really understand

2

what was going on there most of the time, and the sermons he heard meant nothing to him. He was very sure that there was no God.

The carpenter's Bible

Richard grew up and became a businessman in Bucharest. By the time he was in his mid-twenties he had plenty of money. He led a wild life, and this—combined with his earlier lack of good food and poor living conditions— brought on a serious disease called tuberculosis. He nearly died from it and had to spend a long time recovering in a sanatorium, a special hospital where the disease was treated. The disease made him very weak and, after leaving the sanatorium, Richard went to rest and recover in a mountain village. Here he became friendly with an old carpenter, who one day gave him a Bible.

As he was resting Richard had plenty of time to read. He began to read the New Testament and, in his own words, "In the days that passed, Christ seemed to me as real as the person who brought me my meals." So Richard became a Christian.

This happened exactly six months after his marriage to Sabina, a young and very pretty girl. She became a Christian a little while later, not long before she gave birth to their first and only son, Mihai. Such was the change in Richard's life that he decided to become a church minister. After studying, he became a minister of the Lutheran Church, which is a Protestant Church something like the Church of England.

Richard was first arrested in the early 1940's. It was during a reign of terror when a group of people called Fascists governed Rumania. The Fascists were people rather like Hitler. They punished people simply for being

Jews or Protestants—and Richard was both! He was a Jew by race and a Protestant in religion. Three times he was arrested and imprisoned by the Fascist secret police, who were known as the 'Iron Guard' and were very cruel.

Communism

In August 1944 Russian troops invaded Rumania as part of the war against Hitler. The Fascists fell from power, and the Russians forced the Rumanians to have a Communist government like the one in Russia. Then began a nightmare which made the previous sufferings seem easy.

Communism first came to power in Russia. Here there were once a few very rich and very selfish people, while millions of ordinary people were terribly poor and badly treated by the rich. Then there was a revolution in 1917. People thought that a Communist Government would make everything fair for everybody. But unfortunately, because people are selfish and leaders always want power for themselves, Communism has not worked the way people thought it would. It always seems to end up as a police state. That is what happened in Rumania also.

Christians have a specially bad time, because Communism teaches that religion is a bad thing, and must be wiped out. It teaches that there is no God.

Communist governments do not allow the same freedom as we have in this country. We have the right to say exactly what we think and to voice our opinions. Our newspapers can print almost what they want. People can criticise the Prime Minister and other political leaders. Also people can believe in God, and teach others about him if they wish. Ministers can preach what they like and children can go to church and Sunday School if they wish.

This is not so, however, in most countries which are

Russian soldiers in Red Square, Moscow

governed by Communists. They do not allow criticism of the government or freedom to state opinions in public if those opinions are in favour of religion. They allow churches to exist, but only on certain conditions. Church members are not allowed to persuade others to join the church, to give away or sell Bibles and books about Christianity, or to organise Sunday Schools or youth meetings. Also, Church ministers usually have to be approved by the Communist government.

Russian soldiers

Although Richard Wurmbrand was the minister of the Lutheran Church, most of his work was done secretly amongst Rumanians who did not normally attend church, and the Russian soldiers themselves. To talk about Christianity and hand over Bibles to such people was, of course, against the law, but Richard took the risk.

On one occasion he read to a Russian officer the story of how Jesus had been nailed to the cross, and then came alive again. The soldier had never heard of this before and became quite excited. When the story was finished, he was very amazed. He thought the Resurrection was so wonderful that he danced round the room shouting, "He's alive! He's alive!"

Then he fell to his knees and prayed,

"Oh God, what a fine person you are! If I were in your place I would never have forgiven people like me their sins. But you really are a very nice person! I love you with all my heart."

One Russian soldier who became a Christian as a result of Richard speaking to him about Jesus was called Piotr (Peter). Richard had spoken about the story found in the twenty-fourth chapter of Luke's Gospel: the one about how

Jesus met the two disciples who were travelling towards Emmaus. In the story, when they came near to the village, instead of stopping, Jesus was going to continue his journey. Piotr wondered why this was. Surely Jesus wanted to stay with His friends?

"My explanation," said Piotr, "is that Jesus was being polite. He wished to be very sure that he was wanted. When he saw that he was welcomed, he gladly entered the house with them. The Communists are not polite. They enter into our hearts and minds by force. They make us listen to them from early morning till late at night. They do it through their schools, radio, newspapers, posters, films, meetings and everywhere you turn. You have to listen all the time to their godless teaching, whether you like it or not. But Jesus respects our freedom. He gently knocks at the door. Jesus has won me by his politeness." This big difference between Christianity and Communism persuaded Piotr to become a Christian.

Those Christians who talk about Christ and meet together for worship secretly are known as the 'Underground Church'. There is an Underground Church in almost all Communist countries. As this is against the law of these countries, if the Christians are discovered they suffer imprisonment, beating, drugging, threats and blackmail. In this way the police try to persuade those arrested to give up their religious beliefs and to reveal the names of their fellow-believers in the Underground Church.

Arrested

Richard worked both officially as minister of the Lutheran Church and secretly in the Underground Church. That is why he was arrested in 1948.

Thousands of Christians, including Richard's wife, were arrested and imprisoned at around the same time—not only ministers and older people, but also young boys and girls who went to church. The prisons were full, and in Rumania (as in all Communist countries) to be in prison sometimes means to be tortured. However, after a time, Richard's wife and many other Christians were released again.

Every few days Richard was taken out of his cell to be questioned by men called prison interrogators. It was their job to try to obtain information from prisoners. Richard was asked to write an account of his life and his activities, and then he was questioned about it. He was told to write down the names of everyone he knew, the places where he had met them and what his connection or relation with them was. Care was essential, for there were many friends who had helped him in his Christian work. Richard wanted to protect them. Yet if he left out their names and the police knew he had met them, they would almost certainly come under suspicion and be arrested.

For months of questioning Richard refused to admit that he had done anything wrong, or to reveal any of the activities of his Christian friends. Then conditions became tougher for him. His bed was removed from his cell and during the night guards kept waking him up, as he dozed off on his chair. The idea of this was to make him so tired that he would give in and tell the Communists exactly what they wanted. Yet still he told them nothing.

Torture
Then Richard was taken to a room where clubs, truncheons and whips were kept. Here he met one of the torturers, Major Brinzaru, who had hairy arms like a gorilla. The

A secret meeting of the underground church. Why do you think the people's eyes have been blacked out?

torture began. First, he was made to stand for hours facing a wall, with his hands raised high above his head. Long after his arms had lost all feeling and his legs had begun to tremble and then swell, he would collapse on the floor. After being given a crust and a sip of water he would be forced to stand again. At other times he was made to keep walking round and round his small cell, not just for a few hours but for days and nights.

Richard began to suffer once more from tuberculosis. He became very ill and was taken to a prison hospital. Soon he was moved again, this time to a sanatorium. Here he was examined by a friendly doctor, who told him that he had only about two weeks to live. He was taken to the 'death room' where only dying patients were put. For thirty months he lay in the 'death room', and was the first patient ever to leave it alive.

Richard underwent many physical tortures during his imprisonment. For example, sometimes handcuffs with sharp nails on the insides were put on his wrists. If he was completely still they did not cut; in an unheated prison cell in winter, when he shivered with cold, they tore his wrists. On other occasions, he was placed in a wooden cupboard which was only slightly larger than he was and gave him little room to move. Dozens of nails were then driven into the sides of the cupboard, with their razor-sharp points coming right inside. Again, if Richard stood absolutely still it was all right; when he became tired and sagged at the knees, the nails pierced his body.

Another form of torture was being thrown into a cell which had been made into an ice-box, like a large re-frigerator. It was so cold that frost and ice covered the inside. A prison doctor would watch through a tiny open-ing. When he saw signs of Richard freezing to death he would inform the guards and they would rush in and drag Richard out. When he was warm again the guards would put him back into the ice-box. Several times this would happen, thawing out, freezing almost to death and then thawing out again.

Brainwashing

There was also mental torture. For nearly three years Richard was kept in solitary confinement. His only visitor was a guard who brought him black bread and watery soup and who never spoke to him. Imagine not talking to anyone for so long! What could Richard do to avoid going mad? Well, he decided to pray for two hours at a time, to preach sermons to himself, to pretend to be talking

with his wife and son and to dream what he would do if he were a millionaire, the leader of a nation, had the ability to fly like a bird or was invisible. He told himself jokes and invented new ones. He played chess with himself using pieces made from bread: black versus less black! He composed songs and sang them quietly to himself. He even danced!

Then there was brainwashing. For seventeen hours a day—for days, weeks and months—Richard would hear a recorded voice saying over and over again such statements as:

> Communism is good!
> Christianity is stupid!
> Give up!
> Nobody loves you now!

Prisoners were also compelled to listen to talks which praised Communism and ridiculed religion and non-Communist countries.

After eight and a half years of imprisonment, during which time he suffered many broken bones, was burned, and had eighteen holes cut in his body, Richard was released. Immediately he continued his work in the Underground Church. Nearly three years passed before Richard was again discovered in his illegal activities and was imprisoned once more.

Prison again

This second long term of imprisonment, which began in January 1959 and lasted five and a half years, was in some ways worse than the first. He was physically much weaker and less able to endure severe beatings. The food was

Pastor Richard Wurmbrand

terrible—often he was given no more than one slice of black bread a week and one daily bowlful of dirty soup.

During his fourteen years of imprisonment Richard saw much that was horrible. He saw Christians with heavy chains weighing 50 lbs on their feet, being terrified and tortured with red-hot iron pokers. He saw them having spoonfuls of salt forced down their throats and afterwards being refused water.

Many Christians preferred to die rather than give up their faith or do things which were against their conscience. One Christian whom Richard met in prison was called Matchevici. He had been imprisoned when he was eighteen, and because of the tortures and sufferings he had endured he was now very ill with tuberculosis. His family found out about his illness and sent to the prison one hundred bottles of special medicine which might have saved his life. The chief prison officer showed Matchevici the medicine and promised to give the bottles to him if he would provide information against his fellow-prisoners. Matchevici refused. He never received the medicine and it was not long before he died. Richard shared a cell with him and saw him die. The amazing thing was that Matchevici died thanking God for his goodness and love.

God helped and encouraged those who suffered for Him. There was a spirit of real friendship amongst the prisoners, whatever their beliefs, age or background. There was much singing in the cells, even though it was against prison rules and one could expect a beating for it. For the Christians there was also the joy of being able to tell other prisoners, the police and the prison guards about Jesus Christ.

Free at last

In the summer of 1964 Richard, along with several

ПРИЧТЕН К ЗЛОДЕЯМ

"... ПОНОШЕНИЕ Христово
ПОЧЕЛ БОЛЬШИМ ДЛЯ СЕБЯ
БОГАТСТВОМ ..." Евр. 11. 26

**КРЮЧКОВ
ГЕННАДИЙ КОНСТАНТИНОВИЧ**

Стенд уголовного розыска.
Вверху, крайний справа - Председатель Совета
Церквей ЕХБ Крючков Геннадий Константинович
/фотокопия/

/ ДЕТАЛЬ СТЕНДА /

КРЮЧКОВ Геннадий Константинович неоднократно избран на Всесоюзных
совещаниях ЕХБ Председателем Совета Церквей.
На протяжении 10 лет брат Г. К. Крючков мужественно защищает дело
Евангелия в нашей стране.
За верность Господу отбыл срок заключения в лагерях с 1966 по 1969 г.
В настоящее время подвержен особому преследованию со стороны органов
власти, как Председатель Совета Церквей.
За Слово Божие и верность Господу органами власти причтен в разбойни-
кам и злодеям, о чем свидетельствует данный стенд.
На Геннадия Константиновича объявлен всесоюзный уголовный розыск.
Состав семьи: жена - Лидия Васильевна Крючкова и девять детей.
Старшему - 18 лет, младшему - 10 месяцев, которого отец его еще не видел.

дом. адрес: РСФСР г.Тула пос.Рогожинский
ул. Агеева 32 Крючкова Лидия В.

НЕ ЗАБУДЬ О НИХ ЦЕРКОВЬ!

БЮЛЛЕТЕНЬ №3 1971г. **СОВЕТ РОДСТВЕННИКОВ УЗНИКОВ ЕХБ СССР**
г. МОСКВА

*A street poster in Russia. The wanted man is a leader of the Underground
Church.*

thousand other religious and political prisoners, was freed because of a general pardon in Rumania. He was reunited with his wife and son who had patiently and faithfully waited for him during his years of imprisonment. He became the minister of a small church in Orsova, but most of his time was spent working once again in the Underground Church.

Realising the great danger of a further term of imprisonment, Christians in Norway paid £2,500 to the Rumanian government in order to allow Richard and his family to leave Rumania. Before leaving the country, Richard was called to secret police headquarters and was warned of further trouble if he spoke against Communism. He was threatened with being kidnapped and brought back to a Rumanian prison. He knew that this could happen because at one stage he had shared a cell with a bishop who had been kidnapped in Austria and secretly brought back to suffer torture. He was also threatened with having rumours spread about him which would blacken his name, and even with assassination.

In December 1965 the Wurmbrands left Rumania. After Richard had spent many months in hospital recovering, he began to travel throughout Europe, England and America, as well as making brief visits elsewhere, speaking about his experiences and spreading news about the Underground Churches in Communist lands. There are already Christian organisations in nearly sixty countries, whose aim is to help people in Communist lands: they pray for people there, especially all who are suffering; they send money and clothing for the families of Christians in prison; they send Bibles for the many Christians, who have none; they send money so that Christian ministers can travel round to do their work.

When Richard was released from his first long spell in

prison in 1956, one of the first questions his son, Mihai, asked him was, "What have you learnt from all your sufferings?" "Four things were always in my mind," Richard replied. "First, that there is a God. Secondly, Christ is our Saviour. Thirdly, there is eternal life. And fourthly, love is the best way."

Suffering has not made Richard bitter or resentful. It has not made him doubt that there is a God who cares for each one of us. Instead, it has deepened his Christian faith and made him more loving towards others.

BIOGRAPHICAL NOTES

Richard Wurmbrand was born in Bucharest, the capital of Rumania, in 1912, a short while before the First World War (1914–18). His parents were Jewish, but did not actively follow the Jewish faith. His father died when Richard was only nine years old.

He married his wife Sabina in his mid-twenties; they had one son, Mihai, who is now grown up.

Richard Wurmbrand became a Christian when he was 27 years old, and became a minister of the Lutheran Church at about the beginning of the Second World War (1939–45). At this time the Fascists ruled Rumania and supported Hitler.

The Russians invaded Rumania in 1944 and soon after set up a Communist Government.

Richard Wurmbrand was first arrested and imprisoned by the Communists from 1948–56; his second imprisonment by them lasted from 1959–64. Even today he still bears the scars of eighteen deep torture wounds in his body.

He left Rumania with his wife and son in 1965, and first went to Norway, where he spent a time in hospital. The following year he went to America where he still lives, although he travels to many countries speaking about his experiences.

In 1966 he founded the organization called "The Christian Mission to the Communist World", to help Christians in Communist countries. This is his main work today, although ill-health and increasing age mean that his son Mihai does much of the work.

He has written a number of books about the persecution of Christians in Communist countries, and is recognised as a man who can speak with authority about this subject.

ACKNOWLEDGEMENTS: The cover photograph is reproduced by courtesy of Pastor Richard Wurmbrand.
Other photographs are reproduced by courtesy of Associated Press (p. 5) and JTTCW Inc.

THINGS TO DO

A Test yourself
Here are some short questions. See if you can remember the answers from what you have read. Then write them down in a few words.

1 In which year was Richard Wurmbrand first arrested by the Rumanian secret police?
2 Which religion and race did Richard's parents belong to?
3 What did Richard spend his money on when a young man?
4 Which bad illness did he catch?
5 Who first gave Richard a copy of the Bible?
6 Who put Richard in prison the first time?
7 What is the 'Underground Church'?
8 Why did the Communists try to make Richard so tired in prison?
9 How many years did the Communists keep Richard in prison altogether?
10 Who paid the money for Richard and his family to leave Rumania?

B Think through
These questions need longer answers. Think about each question and try to write two or three sentences in answer to each.

1 Why did Richard find it difficult to believe in God when he was a young man?
2 What happened when Richard started reading the New Testament?
3 Why did the Russian Officer think that God was such a "fine person"?
4 Why did Piotr (Peter) like Jesus better than the Communist teaching?
5 What did Richard Wurmbrand learn in prison?
6 What can people in this country do to help Christians in Communist countries?

C To talk about
Here are some questions for you to talk about with each other

Try to give reasons for what you say or think. Try to find out all the different opinions which people have about each question.

1 Why do you think that people in this country do not believe in using torture these days? Can the use of torture ever be right?

2 Some people say that the Christians were the first Communists. Read Mark 10, verses 17–21 and Acts 2, verses 44–45. Do you agree? In what ways are Communism and Christianity similar? In what ways do they differ? Why are Communist governments so opposed to Christians spreading their faith?

3 Suffering sometimes seems to bring out the best in people. Do you think that suffering can be good for us?

4 Why do people suffer? Is it right to blame God? How can people still believe in God when there is so much suffering in the world?

5 Can you explain what changed Richard Wurmbrand's beliefs? How did he change from an atheist (a person who does not believe in God) into a Christian minister who was willing to suffer for his faith?

6 The Communists in Rumania believed they had the truth. If we believe we have the truth, should we try to use force to persuade others?

D Find out

Choose one or two of the subjects below and find out all you can about them. History books, geography books, encyclopaedias and newspapers may be useful. Perhaps you can use reference books in your library to look up some of the names and places.

1 *Rumania* Copy a map of the country from your atlas and mark Bucharest, the capital city. Find out all you can about the country and its people.

2 *Tuberculosis* How do people catch it? Is it common in this country today? In which countries is it still a serious problem? How is it treated?

3 *Communism* Who were Karl Marx and Lenin? Which countries have Communist governments today?
4 *Martin Luther and the Lutheran Church* Who was Martin Luther? In which countries are there large Lutheran churches today?
5 *Christians in Communist countries* Watch out for newspaper articles about them. Read one of the books in the list at the end.

USEFUL INFORMATION

Addresses

News-sheets and magazines giving up-to-date news about Christians in Communist countries can be obtained from:

European Christian Mission, Heightside, Newchurch, Rossendale, Lancs.

Christian Mission to the Communist World, P.O. Box 19, Bromley, Kent BR1 1DJ

Jesus to the Communist World Inc. Box 11, Glendale, California, U.S.A.

N.B. Remember to enclose a stamped, addressed envelope for the reply. A postal order for 25p would also be helpful, if you want plenty of material.

More books to read

Tortured for Christ, by Richard Wurmbrand (Hodder & Stoughton)
In God's Underground, by Richard Wurmbrand (W. H. Allen & Co., Ltd., 1968; Hodder and Stoughton, 1969).
Soviet Saints, by Richard Wurmbrand (Hodder & Stoughton).
The Pastor's Wife, by Sabina Wurmbrand (Hodder & Stoughton).
Tortured for His Faith, by Haralan Popov (Marshall, Morgan & Scott).
Faith on Trial in Russia, by Michael Bordeaux (Hodder & Stoughton).
Two booklets (15p each) available from the European Christian Mission and published by the Heightside Press:
Russian Christians on Trial and *A Criminal Becomes a Christian in a Russian Prison*

Film

A Bitter Cup, from The Christian Mission to the Communist World. A sound-colour documentary about religious persecution in Russia.